1935 if yo[...]
read a good b[...]
either a lot of money or a library card.
Cheap paperbacks were available, but their
poor production generally mirrored the quality
between the covers. One weekend that year,
Allen Lane, Managing Director of The Bodley Head,
having spent the weekend visiting Agatha Christie,
found himself on a platform at Exeter station trying to
find something to read for his journey back to London.
He was appalled by the quality of the material he had to
choose from. Everything that Allen Lane achieved from that
day until his death in 1970 was based on a passionate belief
in the existence of 'a vast reading public for *intelligent*
books at a low price'. The result of his momentous vision
was the birth not only of Penguin, but of the 'paperback
revolution'. Quality writing became available for the price of
a packet of cigarettes, literature became a mass medium
for the first time, a nation of book-borrowers became a
nation of book-buyers – and the very concept of book
publishing was changed for ever. Those founding
principles – of quality and value, with an overarching
belief in the fundamental importance of reading –
have guided everything the company has
done since 1935. Sir Allen Lane's
pioneering spirit is still very much alive
at Penguin in 2005. Here's to
the next 70 years!

MORE THAN A BUSINESS

'We decided it was time to end the almost customary half-hearted manner in which cheap editions were produced – as though the only people who could possibly want cheap editions must belong to a lower order of intelligence. We, however, believed in the existence in this country of a vast reading public for intelligent books at a low price, and staked everything on it'
Sir Allen Lane, 1902–1970

'The Penguin Books are splendid value for sixpence, so splendid that if other publishers had any sense they would combine against them and suppress them'
George Orwell

'More than a business … a national cultural asset'
Guardian

'When you look at the whole Penguin achievement you know that it constitutes, in action, one of the more democratic successes of our recent social history'
Richard Hoggart

Forgetting Things

SIGMUND FREUD

PENGUIN BOOKS

PENGUIN BOOKS

Published by the Penguin Group
Penguin Books Ltd, 80 Strand, London WC2R ORL, England
Penguin Group (USA) Inc., 375 Hudson Street, New York, New York 10014, USA
Penguin Group (Canada), 10 Alcorn Avenue, Toronto, Ontario, Canada M4V 3B2
(a division of Pearson Penguin Canada Inc.)
Penguin Ireland, 25 St Stephen's Green, Dublin 2, Ireland
(a division of Penguin Books Ltd)
Penguin Group (Australia), 250 Camberwell Road, Camberwell, Victoria 3124,
Australia (a division of Pearson Australia Group Pty Ltd)
Penguin Books India Pvt Ltd, 11 Community Centre,
Panchsheel Park, New Delhi – 110 017, India
Penguin Group (NZ), cnr Airborne and Rosedale Roads, Albany,
Auckland 1310, New Zealand (a division of Pearson New Zealand Ltd)
Penguin Books (South Africa) (Pty) Ltd, 24 Sturdee Avenue,
Rosebank 2196, South Africa

Penguin Books Ltd, Registered Offices: 80 Strand, London WC2R ORL, England

www.penguin.com

The Psychology of Everyday Life first published 1901
This translation first published in Penguin Books 2002
This extract published as a Pocket Penguin 2005

1

Copyright 1941 by Imago Publishing Co., Ltd., London
Translation copyright © Anthea Bell, 2002
All rights reserved

Set in 11.5/13.5pt Monotype Dante
Typeset by Palimpsest Book Production Limited
Polmont, Stirlingshire
Printed in England by Clays Ltd, St Ives plc

Contents

Forgetting Impressions and Intentions

Should anyone feel inclined to overestimate the present state of our knowledge of the life of the mind, one need only mention the function of memory to induce a sense of humility. No psychological theory has yet succeeded in giving a full account of the basic phenomena of remembering and forgetting. Indeed, overall analysis of what can in fact be observed has hardly begun. Perhaps we find forgetfulness more of a riddle than memory today, now that the study of dreams and of pathological cases has shown that something we thought long forgotten can suddenly surface in the memory again.

However, we are now in possession of a few insights which may be expected to be generally acknowledged. We assume that forgetting is a spontaneous process involving a certain lapse of time. We emphasize the fact that when something is forgotten, a kind of selection is made from among the available impressions, and that the same thing happens with the details of any impression or experience. We know some of the conditions for the tenacity of certain memories and for the possibility of retrieving a memory that would otherwise be forgotten. However, countless occasions in everyday life show how incomplete and unsatisfactory our knowledge of the subject is. One has only to listen to two people who have received external impressions together, for instance on a journey in each other's company, and who are exchanging memories some time later. An incident that has lodged firmly in the mind of one of them has often been forgotten by the other as completely as if it had never been, even when there is no reason to claim that the impression was any more psychically significant for one than the other. A considerable number of the factors determining what the memory selects obviously still elude our understanding.

With the intention of making a small contribution to our knowledge of the causes of forgetfulness, I am in the habit of subjecting my own instances of forgetting to psychological analysis. As a rule I study only a certain group of these cases, those in which I am surprised to find I have forgotten something because I would have expected to know it. I will just add that I am not inclined to forgetfulness in general (I mean to forgetting experiences, not to forgetting something I have learnt!), and I was capable of unusual feats of memory for a short time in my youth. When I was a schoolboy I thought it quite natural that when I had read a page of a book I could recite its contents by heart, and shortly before going to university I was able to write down popular lectures on scientific subjects almost word for word directly after hearing them. I must still have been using what remained of that ability during the stressful period before my last oral examination for my doctorate of medicine, since I almost automatically gave the examiners answers in some subjects faithfully echoing the text of a book that I had once leafed through in great haste.

Since then my ability to gain access to what is stored in my memory has deteriorated, but until quite recently I have been able to convince myself that with the aid of a certain trick I can remember far more than I would otherwise have thought I could. For instance, if a patient in my consulting rooms mentions that I have seen him before, and I cannot remember when, or indeed recollect meeting him at all, I try guessing, that is to say, thinking quickly of a number of years running from the present backwards. Where written notes or the patient's own certainty make it possible for me to check my ideas, it turns out that I am seldom wrong by more than six months within a period of over ten years.[1] It is much the same when I meet someone I do not know particularly well, and for the sake of politeness I ask how his small children are. If he tells me about their progress then I try to work out

3

how old the child is now, check that age against what the father says, and I am wrong by a month at the most, or three months with older children, although I cannot say what points of reference I used for making my estimate. Recently I have felt bold enough to bring out my guess spontaneously, so as to run no risk of hurting the father's feelings by revealing my ignorance of his offspring. In this way I extend my conscious recollections by calling on my unconscious memory, which in any case contains far more material.

I will therefore give an account of *striking* examples of forgetfulness, most of them observed in myself. I distinguish the forgetting of impressions and experiences, that is to say things I have seen or done, from the forgetting of intentions, that is to say, omitting to do something. I will begin by stating the uniform result of a whole series of observations: *in all cases the motive for forgetting something proved to be based on aversion.*

A) Forgetting impressions and knowledge

1) One summer my wife made me very cross, although the reason was harmless in itself. We were sitting at the *table d'hôte* opposite a gentleman from Vienna whom I knew, and who obviously remembered me too. However, I had my own reasons for

not reviving our acquaintance. My wife, who had heard only the well-known name of the man opposite, made it too obvious that she was listening to what he said to his neighbours at table, for she turned to me from time to time with questions referring to the theme of their conversation. I grew impatient and finally short-tempered. A few weeks later, I was complaining to a woman relative about my wife's conduct, but I could not remember a single word the man had said. As I am usually rather inclined to bear a grudge, and do not forget any of the details of an incident that has annoyed me, my amnesia in this case was probably motivated by consideration for my wife. A similar thing happened to me only recently. I was going to invite a close friend to laugh at something my wife had said just a few hours earlier, but found that I could not put this intention into practice because, remarkably, I had completely forgotten what it was. I had to ask my wife herself to remind me. It is easy to see that this forgetfulness of mine should be regarded as analogous to the typical disruption of the powers of judgement we encounter in dealing with members of our immediate family.

2) A lady who had just arrived in Vienna and did not know the city wanted a small iron safe in which she could keep documents and money, and I had said I would get her one. When I made this offer the unusually vivid image of a shop window in the

inner city where I must have seen such safes came before my mind's eye. I could not remember the name of the street, but I felt sure I would find the shop on a walk through Vienna, since my memory told me I had passed it countless times. To my annoyance, however, and although I combed the inner city, I could not find the shop with safes on display. There was nothing for it, I thought, but to get the names of manufacturers of safes from the addresses in a trade directory, and then go round the area again to identify the shop window I was looking for. However, there was no need for all that; among the addresses listed was one that I could instantly identify as the shop I had forgotten. It was true that I had passed the display window countless times – every time I visited the M. family, who had lived in the same building for years. But now that we were no longer close friends, and indeed were not on good terms at all, I was in the habit of avoiding both the area and the building without stopping to wonder why. On that walk of mine through the city in search of the display of safes I had gone down every other street in the area, avoiding only this single one as if it were forbidden. The aversion motivating my poor sense of direction in this case was palpably obvious. The mechanism whereby I forgot, however, was less simple than in the first example. My dislike was not, of course, for the safes manufacturer, but for someone else whom I did not want to think about, and it transferred itself from that other person to the present occasion, causing me to forget. In exactly the same way, as in the *Burckhard* case, my resentment of one person had caused a slip of the pen in the name of another. The effect of their identical names in that case, linking two essentially different trains of thought, had its parallel in spatial contiguity and indissoluble proximity in the example of the display window. In fact this latter case had a firmer factual basis; there was a second link, one of content, since money had played some part in the reasons for my estrangement from the family living in that building.

3) I was called in by the firm of B. & R. to give medical advice to one of its employees. On the way to his home I was preoccupied by the idea that I must have been in the building where the firm had its offices many times before. I felt that I had noticed the nameplate on a lower floor while I was visiting a patient on a floor higher in the same building, but I could remember neither what the building was nor whom I had been visiting there. Although the whole thing was trivial and unimportant, I could not get it out of my mind, and finally, trying to take my usual long and circuitous route around the subject by assembling my ideas on it, I worked out that the Pension Fischer, where I have frequently visited patients, is one floor above the offices of

the firm of B. & R. I now knew which building accommodated both the firm's offices and the boarding house, but I still could not think why I had forgotten. I could discover nothing repellent in my memory about the firm itself, or the Pension Fischer, or my patients who lodged there. I suspected that it could not be anything very unpleasant, or I would have been unable to recollect what I had forgotten simply by thinking round the subject without, as in the previous case, calling on other aids. It finally occurred to me that only just now, on my way to visit my new patient, a man had spoken to me in the street, and I had found it quite difficult to recognize him. Months before I had seen this man in what looked like a very serious condition, and had diagnosed progressive paralysis, but then I heard that he had recovered, so my diagnosis was wrong. Or perhaps he was in one of those remissions that do occur in *dementia paralytica*, in which case I would have been right after all! It was this encounter that had affected my memory of the neighbourhood of the offices of B. & R., and my interest in finding out what I had forgotten had been transferred from that case of a doubtful diagnosis. The link associating the two, although slight in terms of content – the man who had recovered contrary to my expectations was also an employee of a large firm which used to send me patients – was another instance of an identical name. The doctor who had been with me when I saw the possibly paralytic patient was called Fischer, like the forgotten name of the boarding house in the same building as the B. & R. offices.

4) *Mislaying* something means simply forgetting where you have put it down, and like most people who have a great deal to do with written papers and books, I know what is where on my desk, and can lay my hands on anything I want. What looks like disorder to other people is, to me, order of what is eventually a historical nature. But why did I recently mislay so completely a catalogue of books which had been sent to me that it simply could not be found? I had intended to order a book advertised in it, *Über die Sprache* [*On Language*], because it was by an author whose lively, amusing style I like and whose knowledge of cultural history and psychological insights I admire. I believe that was the very reason why I mislaid the catalogue. In the usual way, I lend this author's books to my acquaintances for their information, and a few days ago someone returning me a book said: 'His style reminds me very much of yours, and he thinks in the same way too.' The speaker did not know what an effect this remark would have on me. Years ago, when I was younger and needed to establish good contacts, an older colleague to whom I had praised the writings of a well-known medical author said much the same to me. 'Yes, just your style, very

much in your own line.' I was encouraged by this to write to the medical author suggesting we might become acquainted, but was put in my place by a cool reply. And perhaps there were also other and even earlier deterrent experiences behind this one, for I never did find the mislaid catalogue, and was probably prevented by this ominous sign from ordering the advertised book, although the disappearance of the catalogue did not really put any difficulty in my way, since the name of the book and its author were lodged in my memory.[2]

5) Another case of mislaying something deserves our attention because of the circumstances in which the mislaid item was found again. A young man told me: 'A few years ago there were some misunderstandings in my marriage. I felt my wife was too cool, and although I was very ready to acknowledge her excellent qualities we lived together without any tenderness between us. One day she came home from a walk bringing me a book that she had bought, thinking it might interest me. I thanked her for this kind attention, promised to read the book, put it somewhere and couldn't find it again. Months passed by, and now and then I thought of the missing book and tried in vain to find it. About six months later my beloved mother, who did not live with us, fell ill. My wife left our home to care for her mother-in-law. The invalid's condition became serious, and gave my

wife an opportunity of showing herself in her best light. One evening I came home, feeling great admiration and gratitude for what my wife had done. I went to my desk, opened a certain drawer in it without any particular intention, but with a sleepwalker's unerring sense of direction, and at the top of the drawer I found the book that had been missing so long.'

J. Stärcke (op. cit.) gives an account of a case of a mislaid item that greatly resembles this one in its concluding feature: the curious certainty with which the lost item was found.

6) 'A young girl was going to make a collar, but she had spoiled the fabric in cutting the collar out. A dressmaker had to be called in to put her mistake right. When she had arrived, and the girl went to fetch the collar from the drawer where she thought she had put it away, she couldn't find it. She turned the drawer right out, but it was nowhere to be found. Feeling annoyed with herself, and wondering why it had suddenly disappeared and whether perhaps the fact was that she didn't *want* to find it, she realized that of course she was ashamed to let the dressmaker see that she had spoiled something as simple as a collar. Once that had occurred to her she stood up, went to another cupboard, and produced the cut-out collar at once.'

7) The next example of 'mislaying' conforms to a type that is familiar to every psychoanalyst. I

should say that the patient who mislaid something in this instance found the key to the puzzle himself:

'A patient in psychoanalysis whose treatment was to be interrupted by a summer holiday during a period of resistance, when he was not feeling well, put his key-ring down in the usual place, as he thought, on getting undressed in the evening. Then he remembered that he wanted to fetch a few items from his desk in readiness for his departure next day, which was also the last day of his course of treatment, when the fee for it would be due. He had put the money in the desk as well. But he found that his keys had disappeared. He began searching his small apartment systematically and with increasing agitation, but in vain. Since he recognized that "mislaying" the keys was a symptomatic action, and therefore something he had really done with intent, he woke his manservant so that he would have an impartial person's help as he went on with his search. After another hour he gave up, fearing he really had lost the keys. Next morning he ordered new keys from the maker of the cashbox on his desk, and they were provided in great haste. Two acquaintances who went home in the cab with him thought they had heard something clink on the ground as he got out, and he felt sure that the keys had fallen out of his pocket. That evening his manservant triumphantly presented him with the original keys. They were tucked between a thick book and a thin pamphlet (a paper by one of my pupils), which he meant to take away to read on holiday, and were so skilfully concealed that no one would have suspected they were there. He found it impossible to replicate the conceal-ment of the keys to make them equally invisible. The unconscious skill with which an item is mislaid as a result of secret but strong motivation is very reminiscent of the sleep-walker's "unerring sense of direction". Of course his motives were dislike of the idea of interrupting his treatment, and his secret annoyance at having to pay a high fee when he still felt so unwell.'

8) A man, writes A. A. Brill, was urged by his wife to attend a social occasion in which he took no interest. He finally gave way to her pleas and began taking his evening dress out of the chest where it was kept, but then interrupted himself and decided to shave first. When he had finished shaving he came back to the chest, but it was closed and locked, and the key could not be found. It was impossible to get hold of a locksmith, since it was a Sunday evening, so the couple had to excuse themselves from the party. When the chest was opened next morning, the key was found inside. Absentmindedly, the man had dropped it into the chest and then closed the lid. He did assure me, says Brill, that he had done so unintentionally and entirely without his own knowledge, but I knew

that he did not want to go to the party, so there
were reasons for him to mislay the key.

E. Jones noticed that he always used to mislay
his pipe when he had been smoking too much and
consequently felt unwell. The pipe would then turn
up in all kinds of places where it had no business
and where it was never usually kept.

9) An innocuous case in which the motivation
was admitted has been recorded by Dora Müller:

Fräulein Erna A. said, two days before Christmas:
'Guess what – yesterday evening I took out my
packet of spiced biscuits and ate some. I thought
that when Fräulein S. (her mother's companion)
came in to say good night to me I ought to offer
her some, not that I really wanted to, but all the
same I decided I would. Later, when she did come
in and I put my hand out to my little table to pick
up the packet, it wasn't there. When I looked for
it afterwards I found it in my wardrobe. I'd put the
packet in there without knowing it.' There was no
need for any analysis; the narrator was clear about
the connection herself. She had just repressed a
wish to keep all the biscuits for herself, but it made
itself felt all the same, automatically, although in
this case the phenomenon was reversed by her
subsequent conscious action.

10) H. Sachs describes the way he once mislaid
something to avoid having to work. 'Last Sunday
afternoon I was hesitating: should I work, or should

I go out for a walk and pay a call? I struggled with myself for a while, but decided to work. After about an hour I noticed that I had run out of paper. I knew I had been keeping a stack of paper somewhere in a drawer for years, but I searched my desk and other places where I thought I might find it in vain, although I went to a great deal of trouble, rummaging everywhere and looking in between old books and pamphlets and so forth. So I felt I had no alternative but to stop work and go out after all. When I came home in the evening I sat down on the sofa, and half in thought, half absent-mindedly, looked at the bookcase opposite. A drawer in it caught my eye, and I remembered that it was a long time since I had examined its contents. I went over and opened it. On top was a leather folder full of blank paper, and only when I had taken it out and was just putting it in the drawer of my desk did I realize that this was the same paper I had been looking for in vain that afternoon. I should add that although I am not thrifty by nature I am very careful about paper, and keep every scrap that can still be used. It was obviously this habit, nurtured by an instinctive drive, that made me remedy my forgetfulness as soon as the present motive for it had gone.'

11) In the summer of 1901 I once told a friend with whom I used to have lively exchanges of scientific ideas at the time that neurotic problems can

be solved only if we take it as read that individuals are originally bisexual. He replied: 'But I told you that myself two and a half years ago in Br., when we were out for an evening walk, and you wouldn't hear of it at the time.' It is painful to be required to surrender one's claim to originality in that way. I could remember no such conversation, nor what my friend had said. One of the two of us was obviously mistaken, and on the principle of who benefits – *cui prodest?* – it must be me. Over the next week I did in fact remember everything just as my friend had tried to remind me of it. I even remembered what I had replied at the time: 'No, I can't agree with you, and I don't want to get drawn into that line of argument.' But since then I have become more tolerant if I come upon one of the few ideas with which my name can be linked elsewhere in medical literature, and find that I have been given no credit for it.

Criticisms of one's wife – friendship that has turned to its opposite – a mistake in medical diagnosis – rejection by people working along the same lines – borrowed ideas: it can hardly be coincidence that a number of examples collected at random like this require me to face such painful subjects in order to explain them. I suspect that anyone else trying to examine his own forgetfulness for its motives could draw up a similar sample card of unpleasant ideas. The tendency to forget unpleasantness seems to me general; the ability to do so is probably developed to a different degree in different people. Much of the *refusal* to acknowledge something that we encounter in the field of medicine may probably be put down to *forgetfulness*.[3] Our view of such forgetfulness, however, restricts the difference between these behavioural phenomena to purely psychological conditions, allowing us to see the same motive expressed in both ways of reacting. Of all the many examples of the refusal to entertain unpleasant memories that I have seen in relatives of the sick, one remains in my mind as particularly strange. A mother was telling me about the childhood of her nervous son, who was now going through puberty, and said that like his siblings he had wet the bed until quite a late age, something not without significance in a case history of neurosis. A few weeks later, when she wanted to know what stage his treatment had reached, I had occasion to mention the young man's signs of a constitutional disposition to illness, and referred to the bed-wetting she had mentioned in her account of his medical history. To my surprise she denied that either he or her other children ever used to wet the bed, asked me what made me think I knew that, and I finally said that she herself had told me so quite recently, although now she had forgotten it.[4]

Healthy people who are not neurotic also display

many signs of resisting the memory of painful impressions and the recollection of unwelcome ideas.[5] The full significance of this phenomenon, however, can be assessed only with reference to the psychology of neurotics, when it becomes obvious that such an *elementary resistance* to ideas that can arouse unpleasant ideas – a resistance comparable only to the flight reflex in reaction to painful stimuli – is to a great degree responsible for the mechanism producing hysterical symptoms. One cannot protest against the acceptance of such a tendency of resistance by claiming that on the contrary, we often enough find it impossible to shake off the painful memories that pursue us and rid ourselves of such unpleasant emotions as remorse and the pangs of conscience. I am not saying that this tendency to resistance will come into effect everywhere, or that in the interplay of psychic forces it may not encounter factors which are working in the opposite direction for purposes of their own, and can defy it. *A structure of multiple stratified agencies can be seen as the architectonic principle of the mental apparatus*, and it is perfectly likely that the tendency to resistance belongs to a lower psychic agency which can be inhibited by a higher authority. However, it says much for the existence and forcefulness of that tendency when we can derive from it processes such as those in the above examples of forgetfulness. We can then see that a good deal is forgotten for its own sake, and where that is not possible the tendency to resistance shifts its aim and at least causes us to forget something else, something less important but associated with whatever it is that really upsets us.

The view proposed here, that painful memories are particularly apt to be forgotten for good motives, deserves to be related to several areas in which it has so far received insufficient or no attention. For instance, it seems to me that we still do not look at the idea keenly enough in considering the credibility of evidence in a law-court,[6] where the oath a witness has taken is obviously far too easily credited with exerting a purifying influence on the interplay of psychic forces in his mind. It is generally accepted that one must consider such motives as they affect the rise of racial traditions and legends, eliminating incidents painful to national feeling from the memory. On closer examination the way in which national traditions and the individual's childhood memories are formed might turn out to be entirely analogous. The great Darwin's insight into the motive of aversion in causing forgetfulness has become a 'golden rule' for scientists.[7]

False memories can occur when impressions are forgotten, just as they occur in the forgetting of names, and, in this case, when the person affected believes them, they are described as paramnesia. The phenomenon of false memory in pathological cases – and in paranoia, when it acts as a constituent factor in the patient's illusions – has given rise to an extensive body of literature, but nowhere do I find any account of its motivation. Since this phenomenon is also part of the psychology of neuroses it is outside the scope of my subject here. Instead, let me describe a curious example of a false memory of my own, obviously motivated by unconsciously repressed material; the way in which the two were linked is also clear enough.

When I was writing the final sections of my book on the *Interpretation of Dreams* I was on my summer holiday and had no access to libraries and reference books. I was obliged to insert all references and quotations in my manuscript from memory, intending to check them later. In the section on daydreams I thought of the well-drawn character of the poor bookkeeper in Alphonse Daudet's *Le Nabab*, through whom the author was probably describing his own day-dreaming. I thought I clearly remembered one of the fantasies entertained by this man – I called him Monsieur Jocelyn – on his walks through the streets of Paris, and began describing it from memory. When M. Jocelyn boldly stands in the way of a bolting horse in the street and brings it to a halt, the door of the carriage opens, a distinguished personage gets out, presses M. Jocelyn's hand, and says: 'My saviour! I owe you my life. What can I do for you?'

I told myself that I could easily correct any inaccuracies in my account of this fantasy at home, when I had the book to hand. But when I did leaf through *Le Nabab* to compare the passage in print with my manuscript, I was dismayed and abashed to find nothing about any such daydream by a M. Jocelyn, which was not even the poor bookkeeper's name; he was called M. Joyeuse. This second mistake soon provided the key to the first, my false memory. *Joyeux* (the man's surname being the feminine form of the adjective) is the way my own name *Freud* would translate into French. So where did the incorrectly remembered fantasy that I had attributed to Daudet come from? It could be only a product of my own mind, a daydream I had invented myself without being conscious of it, or perhaps I had once been conscious of it and had then entirely forgotten it. It was possible that I had it in Paris, where until Charcot took me into his circle I often enough walked the streets alone and full of longing, in great need of some friend and patron to help me. Subsequently I met the author of *Le Nabab* several times at Charcot's home.[8]

Another case of false memory that proved capable of satisfactory explanation is reminiscent of the phenomenon of *fausse reconnaissance*, which will be discussed later: I had told one of my patients, an ambitious and capable man, that a young student had recently introduced himself into my circle with an interesting paper on 'The Artist: An Attempt at a Sexual Psychology'. When this paper was printed a year and a quarter later, my patient said he could remember it perfectly well, since he had read the announcement of its forthcoming publication somewhere before I had first mentioned it (a month or half a year before), perhaps in a bookseller's advertisement. This notice had come straight to his mind at the time, and he said, moreover, that the author had changed the title, since it was now called not an 'essay' or 'attempt' [*Versuch*] but 'approaches' [*Ansätze*] to a sexual psychology. However, careful questioning of the author and comparison of all the dates involved showed that my patient was claiming to remember something impossible. No advertisement for the work had appeared anywhere before its publication, certainly not a whole year and a quarter in advance. When I refrained from analysing this false memory, the same man came up with a similar but new variation. He thought that recently he had seen a work on *Agoraphobia* in the display window of a bookshop, and tried to get hold of it by consulting all the publishers' catalogues. I was then able to explain why his efforts were bound to be unsuccessful: the work on agoraphobia existed only in his imagination as an unconscious intention, because he was planning to write such a book himself. His ambition to emulate the other man and become a member of my circle through producing a scientific work of that kind had led him to both the first and the second false memory. He then remembered that the bookseller's advertisement which he had used as the basis for his first false memory referred to a work entitled *Genesis, das Gesetz der Zeugung* [*Genesis, the Law of Procreation*]. I was responsible, however, for the change of title that he mentioned, since it was I who had misquoted it myself as *Versuch* instead of *Ansätze*.

B) Forgetting intentions

No other group of phenomena is more suitable than the forgetting of intentions to prove the hypothesis that inattention is not enough to explain a slip in itself. An intention is an impulse to perform an action upon which one has already decided, while postponing its execution to some appropriate time. Now, in the interval of time thus created a change in motivation can occur, a change of such a nature that the intention is not carried out, but it has not been actually forgotten, merely revised and rejected. Forgetting intentions, as we are apt to do every day and in all kinds of situations, is not something we usually explain to ourselves by reassessing our motives. We generally leave it unexplained, or look for some psychological elucidation by assuming that around the time it was to have been carried out, the requisite attention to the subject was no longer present, although it would have been an essential condition for the forming of the original intention and must thus have been available at that time for putting it into practice. But observation of our normal attitude to intentions allows us to dismiss this attempt at explanation as arbitrary. If I form an intention in the morning, meaning to carry it out in the evening, I may be reminded of it several times before then, but it does not have to be consciously present in my mind during the day at all. When the time to carry it out approaches, I shall suddenly remember it, and it will impel me to make the preparations necessary for the intended action. If I go out for a walk taking a letter to the post, as a normal rather than a nervous individual I am not in the habit of clutching it in my hand the whole time, constantly looking out for a letterbox in which to post it; instead, I put it in my pocket, go for my walk, allowing my thoughts to wander as they will, and expect that one of the next letterboxes I see will remind me to put my hand in my pocket and take the letter out. Normal behaviour once an intention has been formed coincides exactly with the experimentally induced behaviour of people to whom 'long-term post-hypnotic suggestion' has been given under hypnosis.[9] This phenomenon is usually described as follows: the suggested intention lies dormant in the person concerned until the time to carry it out approaches. It is then aroused and impels the person into action.

In two situations in life, even lay people realize that forgetting an intention cannot by any means be regarded as an elementary phenomenon incapable of being traced further back, and will conclude that tacit motives exist. The two situations I mean are love and military matters. A lover who misses his rendezvous will not find that an excuse to the effect that, unfortunately, he forgot goes down well with his inamorata. She will not hesitate to retort: 'You wouldn't have forgotten a year ago. You don't love me any more.' Even if he were to resort to the psychological explanation mentioned above and try excusing himself by pleading pressure of business, he would only make the lady – as perceptive by now as any psychoanalyst – reply: 'How odd that business worries never used to trouble you!' The lady will not, of course, deny that he may have forgotten; she will merely think, with some justification, that much the same conclusion – a certain cooling of his ardour – can be drawn from unintentional forgetting as from a conscious excuse.

In the same way, any distinction between unintentional and intentional forgetting is ignored in the army on principle, and rightly so. The soldier *must* not forget what his military service requires of him. If he does forget, even though he knew what he had to do, the motives urging him to do his military duty are opposed by other motives running counter to them. For instance, the man doing a year's military service who tries excusing himself on parade by saying he *forgot* to polish his buttons until they shone can be sure of punishment. But that punishment is as nothing compared to what he would risk if he told his superior officers the real reason for his omission: 'I hate army service and all this wretched drill.' It makes economic sense, so to speak, to use forgetting as an excuse or as a compromise solution to spare himself the punishment he would then incur.

Courtship and army service demand that everything to do with them must be impossible to forget, thus suggesting that it is permissible to forget unimportant things; to forget something important, however, shows that it is being treated as unimportant and is tantamount to denying that it matters at all.[10] The standpoint of psychic evaluation cannot be dismissed here. No one forgets to do something that seems to him important without being suspected of mental disturbance. Our study can therefore cover only the forgetting of more or less trivial intentions; but no intention can be considered entirely unimportant, for in that case it would certainly never be formed at all.

As with the functional disturbances described above, I have collected cases observed in myself of neglecting to do something because I forgot, and have tried to cast light on them. I have found in general that they could be traced back to the intervention of unknown and unadmitted motives – or, one might say, to a *counter-will* implying negativity. In some of these cases I found myself in a situation similar to that of military service, under a compulsion which I had not entirely given up resisting, so that I was making my protest by forgetfulness. For instance, I am particularly apt to forget to send good wishes on birthdays, anniversaries, weddings and professional promotions. I always intend to send congratulations, and am increasingly convinced that I shall not succeed. I am now about to give up that intention and consciously allow the motives resisting it to have the upper hand. While I was in the transitional stage I told a friend in advance, when he had asked me to send a telegram of congratulations on his behalf as well as my own on a certain date, that I would forget both, and not surprisingly my prophecy came true. The reason why I feel unable to offer expressions of goodwill that are bound to sound excessive, since the appropriate phrases do not match the very minor amount of emotion I really feel, is to do with painful experiences in my own life. Ever since realizing that I have often taken other people's words of goodwill at face value, I have felt a dislike for conventional expressions of sympathy, although I can see that they are socially useful. Condolences on someone's death are an exception to my ambivalent attitude; when I have made up my mind to send them I do so at once. Nor is the expression of my feelings inhibited by forgetfulness when it has nothing to do with social duty.

First Lieutenant T. gives an account, from his experience as a prisoner of war, of a case of forget-fulness in which an intention initially suppressed made itself felt as an act of 'counter-will' and led to an unfortunate situation: The highest-ranking officer in a prisoner-of-war camp was insulted by one of his companions. To avoid further problems, he intended to make use of the one form of authority still available to him and have the other man moved to a different camp. Only on the advice of several friends did he decide, against his secret wishes, to refrain and take the conventionally honourable line of a challenge, which was bound to have a number of undesirable consequences. The same morning this commanding officer, under the supervision of the camp guard, had to take the roll-call of the officers. He had known his compan-ions for a long time, and had never before made any mistake in reading out the list. Today, however, he omitted the name of the man who had insulted him, who therefore had to stay behind in the parade square after all his companions had left, until the mistake was cleared up. The forgotten name was in a perfectly obvious position in the middle of a sheet of paper. This incident was regarded by one of the parties concerned as an intentional insult, and by the other as an unfortunate and awkward accident which might well be misinterpreted. However, the protagonist in this drama later read Freud's *Psychopathology* and drew the correct conclusions about what exactly had been going on.'

There is a similar explanation for cases where people forget to carry out actions that they have promised to perform as a favour to someone else, because this conventional duty conflicts with their unadmitted personal opinion of it. In such cases it is usual for only the person who was supposed to do the favour to think that forgetting it is any excuse, while the person who asked him to do it undoubtedly gives himself the correct answer: he isn't interested or he wouldn't have forgotten. Some people are commonly described as forgetful, and are forgiven for it in much the same way as a short-sighted person is forgiven for failing to greet an acquaintance in the street.[11] These people forget all the minor promises they have made, and neglect all the tasks they are asked to perform, thus showing themselves unreliable in small things and suggesting that such minor offences in them should not be taken ill – that is to say, should not be explained by their characters but ascribed to something organic in them.[12] I am not one of them myself, and have had no opportunity of analysing the actions of such people in order to discover the motivation for their omissions by looking at what they choose to forget. However, I cannot help suspecting, by analogy, that unusually great if unadmitted contempt for another person is a motive employing that constitutional factor for its own ends.[13]

In other cases the motives for forgetfulness are not so easy to find, and once discovered arouse more of a sense of surprised dissatisfaction. I noticed in the past that when I was paying a great many visits to sick patients, the only ones I ever forgot were those made to people I was treating free of charge or to colleagues. Feeling ashamed of this, I made it my habit to note down in the morning the visits I was going to make that day. I do not know if any other doctors have adopted this habit in the same way, but it does give some idea of what causes a so-called neurasthenic to write down the information he wants to give the doctor in his notorious 'notes'. He seems to lack confidence in the ability of his memory to reproduce his symptoms. And he may well be right, but what happens is usually this: the patient has described his various complaints and put his questions in a very long-winded way. When he has finished, he pauses for a moment, then brings out his notes and says apologetically: 'I wrote a few things down because I have such a bad memory.' As a rule the notes contain nothing new. He goes over each point again, answering it himself: 'Oh yes, I've already asked you that.' His notes are probably just the demonstration of one of his symptoms: the frequency with which his intentions are disrupted by the intervention of unclear motives.

I shall be mentioning something which afflicts the majority of healthy people I know when I admit that, especially in the past, I have found that I easily forget to return books I have borrowed, keeping them for a long time, and I was particularly inclined to put off paying bills by forgetting them. Not long ago I left the tobacconists where I had made my daily purchase of cigars one morning without paying. It was a perfectly innocent omission, since I am a regular customer there, and could therefore expect to be reminded of what I owed next day. But the small forgetfulness, the attempt to run up a debt, must certainly have been connected with the thoughts about my finances that had been occupying me all the previous day. It is easy to find traces of an ambivalent attitude even in most so-called well-conducted people when it comes to money and property. The baby's primitive greed in trying to grab everything it can (and stuff it into its mouth) may prove to have been only incompletely overcome in general by culture and education.[14]

I am afraid that all the examples above have been rather banal. However, I do not mind referring to matters known to everyone and, by the same token, understood by everyone, since my intention is solely to collect everyday examples and subject them to scientific study. I do not see why the insights that reflect our common experience of life should be denied admission to the category of scientific findings. The essential character of scientific study lies not in the disparity of its subjects, but in its strict approach to the establishment of its findings and in trying to make far-reaching connections.

Intentions of moderate importance are found, in general, to be forgotten when opposed by unclear motives. In even less important intentions, the transference to the intention of a negative counter-will from some other source, once an external association has been established between that other source and the content of the intention, constitutes a second mechanism for forgetting. The following example belongs in that category: I like to use good blotting paper, and on my afternoon walk into the inner city I meant to buy some. But on four successive days I forgot to do so, until I stopped to ask myself why. I found my forgetfulness easy to explain when I had recollected that I am in the habit of writing *Löschpapier* [blotting paper], but in speech I use the alternative term *Fliesspapier*. 'Fliess' is the name of a friend in Berlin who had caused me much anxious and painful reflection on the days concerned. I could not shake off such thoughts, but my tendency to resistance (cf. above, p. 18) was expressed by transference, through the similarity of the word, to my not very important and therefore not very resistant intention.

Direct counter-will and more distant motivation coincide in the following case: in the collection *Grenzfragen des Nerven- und Seelenlebens* [*Borderline Problems of Nervous and Mental Life*], I had written a short essay on dreaming, which summed up the content of my *Interpretation of Dreams*. The publisher, Bergmann of Wiesbaden, sent me a set of proofs and asked to have them back by return, because he wanted to bring the collection out before Christmas. I corrected the proofs that night and put them on my desk, ready to take them out with me next morning. In the morning I forgot, and remembered the proofs only that afternoon when I saw their wrapper on my desk. I continued forgetting to send off the proofs that afternoon, that evening and the next morning, until I pulled myself together and took them to a letterbox on the afternoon of the second day, wondering what the reason for my delay might be. Obviously there was some reason why I did not want to send them, but I could not think what it was. However, on the same walk I looked in on my Viennese publisher, the publisher of the book on dreams itself, ordered something from him, and then said, as if struck by a sudden idea: 'I suppose you know I've rewritten my *Dreams*?' 'Oh, no!' he exclaimed. 'No, don't worry,' I said, 'it's only a brief essay for the Löwenfeld-Kurella collection.' But he was still upset; he feared that my contribution to the collection would harm sales of my own book. I assured him it wouldn't, and finally said: 'If I'd asked you in the first place, would you have forbidden me to publish the article?' 'No, of course not.' I myself think I acted entirely within my rights, and did only what everyone usually does, but it seems to me certain now that I had some reservations about writing the article, along the same lines as the doubts expressed by my publisher, and those reservations had motivated my unwillingness to send off the proofs. They derived from an earlier occasion on which another publisher made a fuss when, unavoidably, I took several pages of text from an earlier work of mine on cerebral infantile paralysis published by another firm, and included them unaltered in my discussion of the same subject in Nothnagel's *Handbuch* [*Manual*]. Once again, there was no good reason for anyone to blame me; on that occasion too I had duly told my first publisher (in fact the publisher of the *Interpretation of Dreams*) what I intended to do. But if I look back yet further in this series of memories, it brings me to an even earlier occasion and a translation from the French, when I really did infringe the rights of intellectual property in a publication. I had added notes of my own to the translated text without asking the author's permission, and a few years later I had reason to think that he was not happy with this unauthorized action of mine.

A proverb revealing the popular knowledge that intentions are not forgotten by chance runs: 'What you forget to do once you will forget to do again.'

Sometimes, in fact, it is difficult to avoid the impression that everything which can be said about forgetting and other slips is already known to humanity and accepted as perfectly natural. How odd, then, that one still has to point out such well-known facts to the conscious mind! Time and again I have heard someone say: Oh, don't ask me to do that, I'm sure to forget! There can then surely be nothing mysterious about the accuracy of the prophecy. The person who made it was aware of intending not to carry out the task, and was merely unwilling to admit to it.

Light is also cast on the way in which we forget intentions by what could be called the forming of false intentions. I once promised a young author to write a review of his brief work, but I put it off because of some internal resistance, of which I was not unaware, until one day his urging induced me to promise that I would do it that very evening. And I seriously intended to do so, but I had forgotten that the same evening I was to write a report which could not be postponed. Once I had recognized my intention as a false one, I gave up the battle against my resistance and told the author that I would not write the review.

Notes

1. During the consultation the details of the patient's first visit on the earlier occasion then usually emerge into my conscious mind.
2. I would suggest similar explanations for many of the coincidental occurrences that have been ascribed, since T. Vischer wrote about them, to 'the malice of objects'.
3. If you ask someone whether he suffered from a syphilitic infection ten or fifteen years ago, it is easy to forget that psychically he will think of this disease in quite different terms from, say, acute arthritis. In the accounts given by parents of their neurotic daughters' medical history it is difficult to distinguish for certain between what they have forgotten and what they are concealing, since everything that might stand in the way of the girl's subsequent marriage is automatically eliminated, that is to say, repressed by both parents. A man whose much-loved wife recently died of a lung infection told me the following case of misleading

medical information, which can be ascribed only to such forgetfulness. 'When my poor wife's pleurisy was still no better after many weeks, Dr P. was called in as consultant. In taking down the history of her case, he asked the usual questions, among them whether anyone else in my wife's family had suffered from pulmonary disorders. My wife said no, and I could not remember any either. When Dr P. left, the conversation turned by chance to excursions out of town, and my wife said, "Yes, and it's a long way to Langersdorf *where my poor brother is buried*." This brother had died some fifteen years earlier after suffering from tuberculosis for several years. My wife had loved him dearly, and often talked to me about him. Indeed, it occurred to me that she herself, when her pleurisy had been diagnosed, had been very anxious and had thought, sadly: *My brother died of lung trouble too*. But now she had repressed the memory to such an extent that even after what she had just said about expeditions to L., she could see no reason to correct what she had told the doctor about her family's medical history. I myself had noticed her failure to remember at the very moment when she mentioned Langersdorf.' E. Jones describes an analogous experience in his work, mentioned already several times above. A doctor whose wife was suffering from a disorder of the lower abdomen, which resisted diagnosis, said as if to comfort her: 'It's a good thing there are no cases of tuberculosis in your family.' The wife, much surprised, replied: 'Have you forgotten that my mother died of tuberculosis, and my sister did not recover from the disease until the doctors had given her up?'

4.   At the time when I was writing these pages I suffered the following almost incredible instance of forgetfulness: on 1 January I was looking through my medical records so that I could send out the invoices for my fees, and in doing so came upon the name of M . . . for the month of June. I could not remember anyone with that name. My surprise grew as I noticed, looking forward through my records, that I had treated this case in a sanatorium, visiting daily for weeks. A doctor does not, a mere six months later, forget a patient whom he has treated in such circumstances. Had the patient been an uninteresting person, I wondered, a paralytic? At last, a note about having received my fee restored all the facts that were trying to elude my memory to my mind. M . . . had been a girl of fourteen, the most remarkable case I had treated the previous year and one that taught me something I am unlikely ever to forget. Its outcome was very painful to me. The child fell sick, unmistakably with hysteria, and swiftly and fundamentally improved under my treatment. But after this improvement the child's parents withdrew her from my care. She was still complaining of abdominal pains, which had featured prominently as a symptom of her hysteria, and two months later she died of cancer of the abdominal glands. The hysteria to which the child was also predisposed had used the formation of the tumour as a cause provoking it, and I, with my mind on the obvious but harmless hysterical symptoms, had

perhaps overlooked the first signs of her progressive and incurable illness.

5. A. Pick has recently gathered together papers by a series of authors ('Zur Psychologie des Vergessens bei Geistesund Nervenkranken', *Archiv für Kriminal-Anthropologie und Kriminalistik* by H. Gross) on the influence on the memory of emotional factors, more or less clearly recognizing the contribution that resistance to unpleasant ideas makes to the memory. None of us, however, has described the phenomenon and its psychological basis as exhaustively and impressively as Nietzsche in one of his aphorisms (*Jenseits von Gut und Böse* [*Beyond Good and Evil*], part II, 68): 'I have done this, says my memory. I cannot have done that, says my pride, and insists upon it. At last it is the memory that gives way.'

6. Cf. Hans Gross, *Kriminalpsychologie*, 1898.

7. Ernest Jones points to the following passage in Darwin's autobiography, which tellingly reflects his scientific honesty and psychological acuteness: 'I had, during many years, followed a golden rule, namely, that whenever a published fact, a new observation or thought came across me, which was opposed to my general results, to make a memorandum of it without fail and at once; for I had found by experience that such facts and thoughts were far more apt to escape from the memory than favourable ones.'

8. Some time ago, one of my readers sent me a little volume from F. Hoffmann's series of books for young people, containing an extensive account of a scene involving a rescue, much like the one I had imagined in Paris. The coincidence even went so far as certain rather unusual expressions that appeared in both sources. The possibility of my having in fact read this book as a boy cannot be rejected. The library of my high school contained Hoffmann's collection and was always ready to lend volumes to the schoolboys instead of other intellectual nourishment. The fantasy that I thought I remembered at the age of 45 as someone else's, and then had to recognize as my own and dating from my 29th year, may therefore easily have been the faithful reproduction of an impression absorbed between the ages of 11 and 13. The rescue fantasy I ascribed to the unemployed bookkeeper in *Le Nabab* was only to pave the way for a fantasy of my own rescue, making my wish for a patron and protector tolerable to my pride. No student of the mind will be surprised to hear that even in my conscious life I have felt great resistance to the idea of being dependent on any protector, and have not borne the few real situations in which something similar has occurred with a very good grace. The deeper significance of fantasies involving such subjects, with an almost exhaustive explanation of their characteristics, has been shown by Abraham in a work entitled 'Vaterrettung und Vatermord in den neurotischen Phantasiengebilden' ['Saving and Murdering the Father in Neurotic Fantasies'], 1922 (*Internationale Zeitschrift für Psychoanalyse* VIII).

9. Cf. Bernheim, *Neue Studien über Hypnotismus, Suggestion und Psychotherapie* [*New Studies of Hypnotism, Suggestion and Psychology*], 1892.

10. In Bernard Shaw's play *Caesar and Cleopatra*, Caesar, about to leave Egypt, torments himself for some time with the idea that he intended to do something and has now forgotten what it was. At last it turns out that what Caesar had forgotten was to say goodbye to Cleopatra! This small incident is meant to illustrate – in complete contrast to the historical facts – how little Caesar thought of the Egyptian princess. (From E. Jones, op. cit, p. 488.)

11. Women, with their subtler understanding of the unconscious workings of the mind, are usually more inclined to be offended if someone fails to recognize and greet them in the street than to think of the obvious explanation: that their acquaintance is short-sighted, or so deep in thought that he or she has not seen them. They conclude that they would have been noticed if they were truly valued.

12. S. Ferenczi says that he himself was 'absent-minded' and notorious among his acquaintances for the frequency and peculiarity of the slips he made. However, the signs of this 'absence of mind' have almost entirely disappeared since he began psychoanalytical treatment of his patients, and found himself obliged to turn his attention to his own ego as well. He thinks that slips are abandoned if one learns to extend one's own responsibility, and therefore he contends, in my view correctly, that absence of mind is a condition which depends on unconscious complexes, and can be cured by psychoanalysis. One day, however, he was blaming himself for making a professional mistake in the psychoanalysis of a patient, and all his earlier symptoms of 'absent-mindedness'

returned. He stumbled several times walking down the street (reflecting the *faux pas* he had made in treating his patient), left his wallet at home, offered a kreuzer too little for his tram fare, did not button up his clothing neatly, and so forth.

13.   On this subject, E. Jones points out: 'Often the resistance is of a general order. Thus a busy man forgets to post letters entrusted to him – to his slight annoyance – by his wife, just as he may "forget" to carry out her shopping orders.'

14.   For the sake of thematic unity I will break into my scheme in this book here, and add to what I have said above by pointing out that human memory is especially selective in financial matters. False memories of having paid something already, as I myself know, are often very persistent. When the intention to make a profit is allowed free rein, over and beyond the major interests of life and thus, so to speak, for fun, for instance in a game of cards, the most honest of men are inclined to make mistakes, fail to remember or calculate properly, and find themselves involved in minor frauds without really knowing how. The psychically enjoyable nature of the game is based in part on such liberties. The proverb saying that a person's real character is revealed in gaming may be admitted, so long as his manifest character is not meant. When head waiters make unintentional mistakes of calculation they are often to be regarded in the same way. Businessmen frequently show a certain hesitation to provide sums of money, pay bills, and so on, in a way that will bring them no profit but can be understood

only psychologically, as an expression of the counter-will to get rid of money. Brill points out, with epigrammatic cogency: 'We are more apt to mislay letters containing bills than checks.' It is in connection with their most intimate and least clearly understood emotions that women in particular show especial aversion to paying a doctor. They have usually left their purses at home, and cannot pay in the consulting rooms; they then regularly forget to send the fee from home, and thus achieve the effect of having been treated free – for the sake of their charms. They pay, as it were, with their glance.

Forgetting Proper Names

In the *Monatschrift für Psychiatrie und Neurologie* for 1898, I published a brief article entitled 'On the Psychic Mechanism of Forgetfulness', and I will summarize its content here as my point of departure for further discussion of the subject. In that article, I subjected the frequent occurrence of temporary inability to remember proper names to psychological analysis, using a telling example drawn from my own self-observation, and I came to the conclusion that this common, and in practice not very significant, case of the failure of a psychic function – the function of memory – casts light on matters going far beyond evaluation of the phenomenon itself.

Unless I am much mistaken a psychologist, asked to explain why we so often fail to remember names which we think we know, would content himself with saying that it is easier to forget proper names than the rest of what our memory contains. He would give plausible reasons explaining the special position occupied by proper names, but he would not suspect that the process had any wider relevance.

My own observation of certain details, which may not be present in all cases but can be clearly identified in some, led me to make a thorough study of the phenomenon of the temporary forgetting of names. In such cases the person concerned does not merely *forget*, but also *remembers incorrectly*. As he tries to remember the names that elude him other names – *substitute* names – come into his mind, and although they are immediately recognized as incorrect they persist in forcing themselves upon him. The process that ought to lead to the correct reproduction of the name he is looking for has, so to speak, become *displaced*, thus leading to the incorrect substitute. The basis of my argument is that in psychological terms this displacement is not merely arbitrary, but follows regular and predictable paths. In other words, I assume that the substitute name or names will relate to the name sought in a way that can be traced, and I hope that if I can succeed in proving this relationship I shall also cast some light on the process which makes us forget names.

In the example that I chose to analyse in 1898, I was trying in vain to remember the name of the Old Master who painted the magnificent frescos of the 'Four Last Things' in Orvieto Cathedral. Instead of the name I wanted – *Signorelli* – the names of two other painters, *Botticelli* and *Boltraffio*, sprang to mind, and were immediately and firmly rejected by my judgement as wrong. When I learned the correct name from another source I recognized it instantly and without any hesitation. My study of the influences and associations that had displaced my ability to reproduce the name in this way – taking me from *Signorelli* to *Botticelli* and *Boltraffio* – led me to the following conclusions:

a) The reason for my forgetting the name *Signorelli* is not to be sought in any special feature of the name itself, or in the psychological nature of the context in which it occurred. The name I had forgotten was just as familiar to me as one of the substitute names – Botticelli – and far more familiar than the other substitute name, Boltraffio, since I could have said hardly anything about the man who bore it except that he belonged to the Milanese school of painting. As for the circumstances in which I forgot the name, they appear to me innocuous, and cast no further light on the matter: I was travelling by carriage from Ragusa in Dalmatia, with a stranger, to a destination in Herzegovina, on the way we began talking about visits we had paid to Italy, and I asked my travelling companion whether he had ever been to Orvieto and seen the famous frescos by *** there.

b) My forgetting the name is explained only when I remember the subject we were discussing immediately before I put this question, and it may be seen as a case of *disturbance of the new subject by its predecessor*. Just before I asked my travelling companion whether he had ever been to Orvieto, we had been speaking of the customs of the Turks who live in Bosnia and Herzegovina. I had told him something I had heard from a colleague who practised medicine among these people, and who said that they usually show both complete confidence in their doctors and a total resignation to fate. If you have to tell them that nothing can be done for a sick patient, they will reply: '*Herr* [Sir], what can I say? I know that if he could have lived, then you would have saved him!' And in these remarks the place-names *Bosnia* and *Herzegovina* and the word *Herr* occurred, setting off a series of associations between *Signorelli* and *Botticelli* or *Boltraffio*.

c) I assume that the train of thought leading from the customs of the Bosnian Turks and so forth could disturb my next idea because before that train of thought reached its end, I had withdrawn my attention from it. I remember that I had been about to tell a second story closely associated in my mind with the first. These Bosnian Turks set a very high value on sexual pleasure, and if anything impairs their sexual faculties they fall into despair, a despair which is in curious contrast to their resignation in the face of death. One of my colleague's patients once said to him: 'Well, you know, *Herr*, without all that, life's not worth living.' But I refrained from mentioning this characteristic of the Turks because it was not a subject I thought suitable for a conversation with a stranger. And I did more: I also distracted my attention from continuing my train of thought along those lines, lines that could have led to the subject of 'death and sexuality' in my mind. At the time I was feeling the after-effect of some news I had heard a few weeks earlier, during a brief visit to *Trafoi*: a patient over whom I had taken a great deal of trouble had committed suicide because of an incurable sexual disorder. I am perfectly sure that I did not consciously remember this sad event or anything connected with it on that journey to Herzegovina. But the similarity of the names *Trafoi* and *Boltraffio* obliges me to assume that at the time, and although I was intentionally distracting my attention from it, this memory was activated in my mind.

d) I can no longer regard the fact that I forgot the name of *Signorelli* as mere chance. I have to recognize the influence of a *motive* in the procedure. I had motives for interrupting myself as I was about to impart my ideas (about the customs of the Turks and so forth) to my companion, and those motives also caused me to block the ideas connected with them, which would have led on to the news I heard in Trafoi, out of my conscious mind. I therefore wanted to forget something; I had *repressed* something. What I wanted to forget was not in fact the name of the painter of the masterpiece in Orvieto, but the other subject, the one I did want to forget, contrived to associate itself with his name, so that my act of volition failed to find its target, and I *unintentionally* forgot one idea while I *intentionally* meant to forget the other. My aversion for remembering was directed against the content of one idea; my inability to remember emerged in another context. Obviously this case would have been simpler if the contexts of my aversion and my inability to remember had been the same. But the substitute names no longer seem to me so entirely unjustified as they were before the context was elucidated; in the manner of a compromise, they remind me of both what I wanted to forget and what I wanted to remember, showing that my intentional forgetfulness was neither wholly successful nor entirely unsuccessful.

e) The way in which I made a connection between the name I sought and the subject I had repressed (death and sexuality, etc., with mention of the names of Bosnia, Herzegovina and Trafoi) is very striking. The diagram I give here, taken from my 1898 article, attempts to illustrate this connection.

The name *Signorelli* has been divided into two. One pair of syllables (*elli*) also occurs unchanged in the substitute name; the other, if we translate

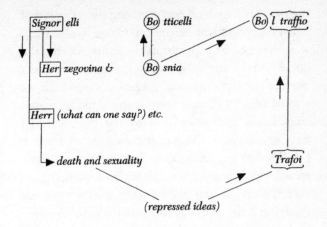

Signor into *Herr*, has a number of different connections with the names belonging to the repressed
subject, but because of those connections it eludes
reproduction. The substitution occurred as if there
had been a displacement of meaning through the
linked names of 'Herzegovina and Bosnia', but
disregarding the sense and the acoustic demarca-
tion of the syllables. In the process, therefore, the
names have been treated like the written characters of a sentence that is to be turned into a rebus
or pictorial puzzle. No understanding entered my
conscious mind of the way in which the substitute
names replaced the name of *Signorelli*. *At first* it
seems impossible to trace any connection – deriving
from the recurrence of the same syllables (or rather
sets of characters) – between the subject in which

the name of *Signorelli* occurred and the subject that I had repressed just before broaching it.

It may not be superfluous to point out that the conditions assumed by psychologists to affect correct reproduction and forgetfulness, which we should seek in certain relationships and predispositions, are not invalidated by the explanation I have given above. Only in some cases can a *motive* be added to the recognized factors that may lead to our forgetting a name, thus also explaining the mechanism of false memory. In the case we are studying here, these predispositions are essential to allow the repressed element to associate itself with the name being sought, and then to repress that name too. The same thing might not have happened with another name, in conditions more favourable to its reproduction. In fact it is likely that a suppressed element is always trying to make itself felt somewhere else, but will succeed in doing so only where it finds suitable conditions. On other occasions, suppression may occur without any disturbance of the functions or, as we might accurately say, without showing any *symptoms*.

To sum up the conditions for forgetting a name and remembering it incorrectly, therefore, they comprise: 1) a certain predisposition to forget that name, 2) a process of suppression which has taken place shortly before, 3) the possibility of establishing an *external* association between the name concerned and the recently suppressed element. The last-named condition need not necessarily be considered very important, since the establishment of some association or other is so easy that it would probably be possible to find one in most cases. However, another question, and one that goes deeper, is whether such an external association can really be sufficient to make the repressed element prevent reproduction of the name being sought, or whether there must not necessarily be some closer connection between the two subjects. At first sight one would be inclined to reject this last requirement and say that the temporal proximity of a subject with an entirely different content is enough. On closer examination, however, it becomes increasingly frequent to find that the two elements (the repressed element and the new one), while linked by an external association, also have some connection of content, and such a connection can indeed be shown to exist in my example of *Signorelli*.

The value of the insight acquired through analysis of the *Signorelli* example of course depends on whether one wants to explain the case as typical or as an isolated instance. I can only say that it is extremely usual for a name to be forgotten and incorrectly remembered in the same way as in the *Signorelli* case which I have set out here. Almost every time I have observed the phenomenon in myself, I have also been able to explain it as being motivated by repression in the way described above. I must also state another point supporting the likelihood that this analysis was typical. I believe that in principle there are no grounds for drawing a distinction between cases in which names are forgotten and incorrectly remembered, and those in which no incorrect substitute names come to mind. Such substitute names occur spontaneously in a number of cases; in certain other cases, where they do not occur spontaneously, they can be made to do so by intense concentration, and they will then show the same connections between the repressed element and the name being sought as they would if they actually had been spontaneous. There seem to be two main factors in the emergence of a substitute name into the conscious mind: first, the effort of concentration, and second, an internal context associated with the psychic material. I might trace the latter to the comparative ease or difficulty of establishing the necessary external association between the two elements. A good many of the cases in which a name is forgotten but no false name is remembered may thus be classed with those cases in which substitute names are produced, as described in the mechanism of the *Signorelli* example. I will not, however, be so bold as to claim that all cases of forgetting proper names can be classified under this heading. There are undoubtedly cases where names are forgotten for much simpler reasons. We shall probably have defined the facts cautiously enough if we say that *while proper names are sometimes forgotten for simple reasons, they are also sometimes forgotten for reasons motivated by repression.*

POCKET PENGUINS